Purple Buttons

ANGELA

Illustrated by Sue Porter

OXFORD
UNIVERSITY PRESS

OXFORD
UNIVERSITY PRESS

Great Clarendon Street, Oxford OX2 6DP

Oxford University Press is a department of the University of Oxford.
It furthers the University's objective of excellence in research, scholarship,
and education by publishing worldwide in

Oxford New York

Auckland Cape Town Dar es Salaam Hong Kong Karachi
Kuala Lumpur Madrid Melbourne Mexico City Nairobi
New Delhi Shanghai Taipei Toronto

With offices in

Argentina Austria Brazil Chile Czech Republic France Greece
Guatemala Hungary Italy Japan Poland Portugal Singapore
South Korea Switzerland Thailand Turkey Ukraine Vietnam

Oxford is a registered trade mark of Oxford University Press
in the UK and in certain other countries

British Library Cataloguing in Publication Data
Data available

ISBN-13: 978-0-19-917964-0
ISBN-10: 0-19-917964-6

3 5 7 9 10 8 6 4 2

Available in packs

Stage 10 More Stories A Pack of 6:
ISBN-13: 978-0-19-917963-3; ISBN-10: 0-19-917963-8
Stage 10 More Stories A Class Pack:
ISBN-13: 978-0-19-917970-1; ISBN-10: 0-19-917970-0
Guided Reading Cards also available:
ISBN-13: 978-0-19-917972-5; ISBN-10: 0-19-917972-7

Cover artwork by Sue Porter
Photograph of Angela Bull by courtesy of the Craven Herald

Printed in China by Imago

Buttons! There's nothing special
about buttons! Rachel never knew
there was, until –

Until she saw Gran's buttons.

Rachel ran into Gran's house
one day.

She had some good news.

'Our class at school is doing a play,' she said. 'I'm going to be the Queen.'

Gran looked pleased.

'What will you wear?' she asked.

'A long dress,' said Rachel, 'and a crown. Our teacher says I can make the crown myself, with gold paper. I can stick fruit gums on for jewels.'

'That sounds silly,' said Gran.
'Queens don't have sweets on their
heads.'

Rachel thought for a minute.

'You're right,' she said. 'But – what
could I use instead?'

'How about buttons?' said Gran.

Buttons!

'They might be good,' said Rachel. 'But I haven't got any.'

'I've got lots,' Gran told her. 'Fetch me the blue tin from the corner cupboard. I'll show you.'

Rachel carried the blue tin to Gran's table. Gran took off the lid, and tipped up the tin.

Out came a shower of buttons.
Rachel had never seen so many! They
rattled and spun and danced over the
table. Rachel had to catch two handfuls
before they rolled on to the floor.

Some were like tiny white daisies.
Some were like big splodgy snowflakes.
There were neat blackcurrants. There
were bright red cherries. There were
pale lilac petals.

And they were all buttons!

'They're lovely!' cried Rachel. She
stopped. 'Most of them,' she said.

She'd seen the purple buttons.

She knew at once that she hated them.

The purple buttons were thin and slippery. They were dark as bruises. They peeked up at Rachel like sly, winking eyes.

'Why have you got these nasty purple buttons, Gran?' Rachel asked.

'I keep all my buttons,' said Gran.
'I cut them off clothes that I've
finished with. There's a story to
every button.'

'Well, I don't like the purple
ones,' said Rachel.

She pushed them away.

'I want some for jewels,' she said.

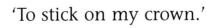   'To stick on my crown.'

She began to pick up the brightest,
shiniest buttons on the table. Some
sparkled like gold. Some gleamed like
silver. Some were warm scarlet. Some
were cool emerald.

'Can I borrow these?' she asked.
'Thank you, Gran. You *are* kind!'

When she got home, she made her gold paper crown. She stuck Gran's buttons along the front. They were just like real jewels.

Everybody admired Rachel's crown.

When the play was over, Rachel took the buttons carefully off the crown. She was thinking. It would soon be her little brother Matthew's birthday.

'Gran,' she said, when she took
the buttons back. 'Can I borrow
some more, please? I want to stick
them on the frill round Matthew's
birthday cake.'

Once more Gran tipped out her
buttons.

'Orange and yellow, I think,'
said Rachel.

She scooped up a handful to choose
from – and dropped them.

Under the bright colours lurked the
purple buttons. They were so ugly!
They winked at Rachel with evil,
goblin eyes.

'Where did you get these horrid
buttons, Gran?' she cried.

'They aren't horrid,' said Gran.

She took a purple button, and looked at it closely.

'I cut them off a dress,' she said. 'I had it when your Grandad was alive. It was a nice dress, but things seemed to go wrong when I wore it.'

'Like what?' asked Rachel.

'Once I broke my ankle,' said Gran.

'Once the car crashed. So I didn't want to wear the dress again. But I snipped off the buttons, and kept them.'

'What for?' said Rachel. She knew *she* would have thrown the nasty purple buttons away.

'You never know. They might come in handy one day,' said Gran.

She smiled, as if she liked the dark purple buttons.

Rachel chose nice bright ones for Matthew's birthday cake.

Not long afterwards, Rachel's mum began to knit a cardigan for her. It was made of warm lilac wool, and it needed four buttons.

'Maybe Gran would lend you some buttons for it,' said Mum.

Rachel thought about Gran's buttons. She remembered the ones that looked like pale lilac petals. They would be perfect.

She asked about them, next time she went to see Gran.

'Is it all right if I borrow your lilac buttons for my new cardigan?' she said.

She fetched the blue tin from the cupboard, and tipped the buttons onto the table. She counted the lilac petals. Yes, there were four! Just right.

'Can I take them home?' she asked.

Gran didn't answer.

Rachel looked at her. Gran was sitting in her chair, with a very sad face.

'Gran!' cried Rachel. 'What's the matter?'

Gran held out her hand.

'It's my ring,' she said. 'I've lost one of the garnets out of it.'

'What are garnets?' Rachel asked.

'Those dark red stones. Can you see that one's missing?'

Rachel stared. There was a gap in the row of jewels on the ring.

'It must have fallen out,' said Gran sadly. 'I've hunted high and low, but I can't find it. And the ring's very special. Grandad gave it to me, forty years ago.'

3

Rachel jumped up. Gran had done
a lot for her. She wanted to do
something back.

'I'll look for it!' she said. 'It can't be
far away.'

Gran shook her head.

'Don't bother,' she said. 'We'll never
find it now. It's so tiny. Maybe it got
swept up in the hoover.'

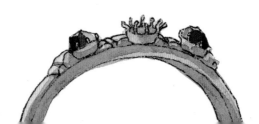

Rachel sat down again. She stared at
the buttons she'd tipped out. Some of
Gran's sadness seemed to have rubbed
off on to them. The white ones looked
dull and wishy-washy. The gold ones
didn't shine any longer. Even the lilac
petals were faded and dim.

Only the purple buttons still glittered on the table. They were thin and strange.

Wicked.

When Gran wore them on a dress, bad things happened. Now, bad things were happening again.

It must be their fault.

'I *hate* the purple buttons!' Rachel cried.

She flicked one as hard as she could. It spun across the room, into a far corner.

'Hey!' exclaimed Gran. 'Stop it! I like my buttons. I don't want to lose them as well as the garnet.'

She looked quite cross. Rachel felt awful.

'Sorry, Gran,' she said.

She flew to the corner where the button had fallen. She ran her hands along the carpet, trying to find it.

Something winked. Something glinted. Rachel peered down. There was the purple button! But it wasn't lying flat. It slanted, as if it was half propped up.

What could it be propped against?

Rachel lifted it with the tip of her finger. Hidden under the button lay a tiny red jewel.

Rachel's heart thumped, as if she'd
run from one end of the playground to
the other. She picked up the jewel and
the button, and held them out.

'Gran! Look!' she said.

'Oh!' cried Gran. 'The garnet from my ring.'

Her face was happy again.

'I found it under the purple button,' said Rachel.

She was smiling too.

'Then it's lucky you flicked the button off the table,' said Gran. 'The nice, purple button.'

'Why do you like it so much, Gran?' Rachel asked.

'Because it's pretty,' said Gran. 'You might think so too, if you looked at it properly.'

For the first time, Rachel looked at the button as hard as she could. Her eyes opened wide with surprise.

'Yes!' she cried. 'It's lovely!'

The button shone with a pale, pearly glow. It's rim was carved like a shell. And it wasn't thin and slippery. It was slim, and smooth, and elegant.

Quickly, Rachel picked up the other purple buttons from the table. She counted them. One, two, three, four. Just right!

'Gran,' she said. 'You know I need four buttons for my new cardigan. Could I borrow the purple ones?'

'Of course,' said Gran. 'Don't forget, I told you they might come in handy one day.'

31

About the author

When I was a little girl, my
mother kept buttons in a
shiny, six-sided tin. As a treat,
she sometimes let me play
with them, sort them out
and make them into
patterns. So I wrote a story
about another girl, Rachel,
who enjoys buttons.

When my own two children were small, I kept
my buttons in a jam jar. Not so interesting!
So now that I've got two grandchildren as
well, I must find a proper, shiny button tin.

I live in the country, and I've written lots of
children's books.